THE HANDBOOK ON HOW TO PROBATE AN ESTATE

TABLE OF CONTENTS

I0462737

IMPORTANT CONCEPTS AND DEFINITIONS

Deceased/Decedent

the person who has just died is called the deceased or decedent for most legal and tax purposes.

Estate

the assets owned or enjoyed by a deceased person which are subject to probate after death.

Will

The last valid document that the deceased signed or executed which directs the disposition of his or her estate. To be valid, a will must have been properly executed. Wills and codicils that are not properly executed may be ruled invalid by the courts. In most states, two witnesses must be available to attest to the maker's signing of the will. This means that they sign the will as witnesses to the maker's signing of his/her will. They may be called upon to testify to the Probate Court that the decedent (the maker) was of sound mind and memory when the will was made.

They must have been with the maker when the will was made and they must know that the maker signed the will. They must also have been made aware at the time that the decedent was making his or her last will and testament. Usually, this is done by the maker or the attorney reading a statement to that effect after the maker has signed the will.

It is very common for the witnesses to also give an affidavit in proof of the will. This affidavit is a sworn, notarized statement indicating that they acted as witnesses to the signing by the maker of the will, that the maker was of full (legal) age and of sound mind and memory at the time of signing and declared that the maker was signing his or her last will and testament, and that the witnesses signed the will as witnesses in the presence of the maker and of each other, and did so at the request of the maker.

Provisions of the Will

Typically, a will is drafted according to an overall pattern, typically numbered by article, for example "Article I", etc.

I.   states that it is intended to be the last, and therefore the only valid will of the deceased.

II.   states that any debts and taxes should be paid out of the assets of the estate.

III. special gifts or particular items of property (or cash), may then be given away to named individuals or charitable organizations.

IV.   the residue or remainder of the estate is next given away.

V.   Then, the person who has made the Will can name an executor of the estate. The executor is the person or persons who are designated to wind up the affairs of the person making the will. The executor will be given certain legal powers. Trustees of testamentary trusts created under will may also be named.

VI.   the will may then state that certain persons are to be appointed to act as guardians of certain dependent persons, e.g. children as well as any property going to such dependents.

VII. Finally, the will is signed and dated by the maker. The witnesses then sign and may also make the affidavit in proof of the will.

Codicil

Amendments to a will are made by codicil. A codicil must be executed like a will, i.e. signed and dated, before two witnesses.

Submission of Will to Probate

A testator's will must be filed with the Probate Court within 30 days from the date of death.

If a person knows of a decedent's will or codicil or has them in his possession, he must inform the Probate Court or the executor named in the will and turn over the documents within 30 days from the date of death. Failure to do so is a crime in many states.

Executor or Administrator

This is the person (an individual or a bank or trust company) who is formally approved by the Probate Court to wind up the affairs of the deceased.

If there is a valid will, then the person appointed is called an executor. If there is no valid will, then the person appointed is called the administrator. There is no practical difference between them, except that the label applied will indicate to others if the estate is being administered according to the terms and conditions of a valid will, or if the deceased died intestate. The words "personal representative" are sometimes used to refer to a person who is acting unofficially for an estate. [Different states may use "personal representative" to designate the official fiduciary.]

Although the probate laws favor the appointment of a close relative (such as the surviving spouse or adult children) to act as executor or administrator, the Probate Court has the authority to appoint someone who is not a relative, or who has not been designated in the will of the deceased. This is because the fiduciary acts under the court's authority and supervision.

Fiduciary

A fiduciary generally is a person who is entrusted with certain legal duties in caring for the property of another person. Executors and administrators are "fiduciaries", as are trustees, guardian, and conservators. It is very important to recognize that fiduciaries have personal liability and may be sued for failure to properly administer an estate or trust. With few exceptions, fiduciaries must regularly account to the court (and to the beneficiaries) for the proper use and application or distribution of estate funds and property. They must be very careful in what they do with an estate.

Executor/Administrator (Fiduciary) Responsibilities

The basic responsibilities of the executor or administrator (fiduciary) are:

1. to manage all transactions of the estate in a careful manner;
2. to preserve the assets of the estate;
3. to expedite the settlement of the estate;
4. to deal fairly and impartially with all beneficiaries and creditors;
5. to file all necessary documents with the Probate Court.

Testator/Testatrix

The deceased (male/female) who left a will.

Probate

In the dictionary definition, probate refers to the action of proving in court that a document is the valid last will of a deceased person.

More generally, it refers to all of the actions or steps needed to be taken in addition to formal admission of the will to finish up and close an estate. If the court finds that a will was properly executed, then the court accepts or "admits" the will for probate. If a person does not have a valid last will, then he or she died "intestate" and his estate will be distributed according to a pattern established by the state's laws of intestacy.

Probate Court

By whatever name may be used in a given state, this is the court that has jurisdiction over probate matters in the area (town, city, county…) in which the decedent permanently resided. If the deceased was not a resident of the state, he is said to have been "domiciled" elsewhere. In that case, any property that he owned or that is physically located in this state is subject to ancillary probate in the town where the property was located.

The Probate Court has legal authority over all decedents estates, whether or not there is a will. A decedent's estate is always subject to some sort of probate supervision. It doesn't matter that there are no assets, if the decedent had debts or taxes due which have to be settled. In all cases, the Probate Court has jurisdiction over the estate and the estate should be brought before the Probate Court. For this reason, known wills must be filed within a certain period after the date of decedent's death, typically within 30 days.

Settlement of Small Estates

For small or very simple estates, there are procedures to simplify or limit the probate process. If there is a will, it must be submitted to the court but probate of an estate that qualifies as "small" can be avoided by filing a "no probate" form or petitioning the court for permission to proceed without formal probate. If the will is inconsistent with the intestacy laws, however, then admission of the will to probate may be necessary.

The threshold defining a "small" estate varies by state, from anywhere between $5000 to $100,000. For example, Georgia allows its probate courts to use its simplified small estate process if there is no will and no debts and all heirs concur as to division of any assets. In comparison, Hawaii allows use of an affidavit process if the total value of all a Decedent's Hawaiian assets does not exceed $100,000; or a simplified probate process may be used at the executor's request. Probate statutes are regularly reviewed to see if the defining threshold needs to be adjusted upwards due to inflation.

Death Taxes

There are different types of death taxes, which arise when a person dies and passes assets to his heirs. The first type is called an estate (or inheritance) tax; the second type is called a succession tax [or inheritance tax]. An estate tax, which is the type levied by the Federal government, is a tax on the value of assets valued on the date of death at the fair market value. A succession tax, which is the type levied by some states, is a tax on the value of the assets passing to a particular class or group of beneficiaries (such as the surviving spouse - Class AA; children and parents - Class A; brothers and sisters - Class B, and so forth.)

An estate tax, like that imposed by the Federal Government, allows a tax exclusion or credit against the tax that is calculated as due. In computing the Federal estate tax, the estate is allowed to deduct a maximum estate tax credit, which under 2010 legislation, is equivalent to passing $5 million (in cash or in value of assets) tax free to a decedent's heirs. (Married couples may pass up to $10 million.)

A succession tax, in contrast, is a tax based not only on the value of assets (usually above a certain threshold amount), but also on which heirs get them. Heirs are classified by how close in the family tree they were to the decedent. For example, property passing to a spouse may not be taxed (the equivalent of a 100% exclusion); whereas property passing to children and/or surviving parents may be entitled to a lesser exclusion (e.g. $50,000); property passing to a cousin or aunt/uncle may get an even smaller ex-exclusion, etc.

STARTING THE PROBATE ESTATE

How to begin the probate estate

When a person dies, those close to the deceased must do several things simultaneously.

1. Give the attending doctor and the funeral director the information they need to prepare the death certificate and prepare for burial or cremation. Depending on the circumstances surrounding the death (accidental or due to illness), other authorities, such as the police, may need information about the deceased's residence, next of kin, etc.. This information will also be used later during probate, so it is important to keep a permanent record at the outset.

2. Arrange the funeral service, memorial, wake.

3. See that bereaved next-of-kin receive proper care.

4. Notify life insurance companies, pensions plans, social security and other payers of death benefits to arrange for payments.

Secure the decedent's assets

It is critically important that the personal representative of the deceased (e.g. those having access to and/or control over the assets, such as the surviving spouse or other family members) secure and safe keep all of decedent's assets. Such assets include all personal possessions, real estate, investments, accounts, collections, etc. that were in decedent's name at the time of death.

To do this, it is necessary first to identify the decedent's assets (see next item).

Since the personal representative is personally liable for preserving such assets, no time can be wasted securing keys and locks to decedent's residence and any other place where Decedent may have kept assets.

Unaccompanied access to such premises should not be given to anyone, at least until an inventory of all property has been completed. Heirs should not be allowed to take any of decedent's property unless and until the personal representative is prepared to formally account for and release such property. Signed and dated receipts for any property given out to heirs or others should be obtained from those receiving such property.

Collect all information and records immediately

Probate requires the gathering of considerable detailed information about the decedent's assets. It is very important to do this as soon as possible! It is a time consuming task. However, pulling together as much information and records as possible at the beginning of the estate will pay off in dividends later on during the probate process.

Understand at the outset that there are no short cuts! What isn't done now and done well will have to be done (or redone) later, if not by you, then by someone else.

Try to be precise and comprehensive. Do not procrastinate. The work only gets harder if it has to be done later. It is very expensive and irritating to have to reconstruct information that is lost or mislaid.

There will probably be many records and documents, albeit poorly organized. Get several large cardboard boxes to hold them. Do not try to sort the records at this time. (Sturdy document storage boxes are best and should be available at your local office supply store. Buy two large black-ink markers and one or two dozen plain white self-sticking labels (minimum size: 4" by 6").

Keep records found in different locations in separate boxes. Use the marker pens to mark the boxes by the area in which you found the records, e.g. "DESK; MASTER CLOSET; SAFE" and so forth. This will help to keep similar records together for later identification and sorting.

1

Look into all desks and table drawers. Search all closets (in boxes or on shelves or at the back of the closet), bookcases, basements, attics and garages. If there is a safe, look for the combination or key.

Sort through the decedent's papers

Put anything that looks important in labeled files in the boxes.

For example, label a file "Bank accounts" and put in it all the savings account and bank statements, checkbooks, savings books and bank certificate of deposit records.

Look for the Decedent's Will and any Codicils

They may be with other papers at the last residence, or in a safe deposit box, or at the decedent's attorney's office.

If you find only a copy, look on the copy for the name of any attorney. Also, look at who is named as executor and, if necessary contact that person to ascertain whether the decedent left the original will with that person.

The original executed will must be submitted to the Probate Court within a statutory period (typically 30 days) from the date of death by anyone having the will in their possession. Even if a will is not submitted for probate, the will must be filed with the court! If an original cannot be found, then the court may have to determine whether a copy can be admitted to probate in place of the original.

Note: If the person in possession of a will neglects to file the will with the Probate Court within the required days from knowledge of the testator's death, he may be subject to fines or prison or both.

Safe keep valuable items

Valuable assets would include securities (stocks, bonds, insurance policies, cash, travelers checks, coins or other collections, artwork, silver, jewelry, and the like. Put them in a safe or bank deposit box opened in the name of the estate (i.e., the John Doe Estate). Do not use a deposit box or brokerage account that is in decedent's name.

Make a descriptive list of such items when you find them! Don't skimp on your descriptions, since you'll have to describe the items in detail in tax returns and court papers.

Helpful Hint: write down all names, addresses and telephone numbers of any brokers, agents, etc., that you see on documents. You may need this information later to trace whether assets are part of the estate and to determine their value.

Locate safe deposit boxes

Check with decedent's bank or trust company to see if they maintained a safe deposit box that is listed under the decedent's name. If you find a safe deposit box key or combination, refer to that in arranging a meeting to open the box.

Decedent's will can be removed from a box, but no other assets if the estate must be probated, in which case a court order is likely to be required even to open any safe deposit boxes to take an inventory. No one except a joint tenant owner of the box* is normally permitted to open a box without a court order. Nothing but the decedent's will can be removed from a box that is opened under such a court order. The bank officer attending the opening must file a return to the court swearing that nothing but the will was removed. Only the fiduciary, once appointed, may close the box and take out the contents, pursuant to the court's authority.

*NOTE: A joint tenant may enter a box and remove the contents. But beware of doing so! Assets in the box may belong to someone else. Also, joint tenants are subject to death taxes and may bear liability for taking assets not belonging to them (e.g. held in the box in trust by the decedent.)

Determine if formal probate of will is necessary.

Even when a decedent has a will, most states have modernized their probate laws to permit heirs to settle qualified small estates without having to go through the formal probate process – using either the affidavit approach or a simplified probate process. They usually apply only to estates in which no known will is presented for probate or no application for administration is filed within 30 or so days after death. There may be other conditions preventing use of a small estate process, for example: (a) that decedent owned no real estate except for property that was owned with another person who has rights of survivorship, e.g. joint and survivor type property doesn't eliminate use of this procedure; (b) that the remaining assets* are not worth more than a certain threshold amount $X; (c) settlement of the estate outside of probate is subject to challenge by disgruntled heirs or creditors.

*Specified assets typically include: i. bank deposits; ii. equity in certain in-state financial institutions; iii. corporate stocks or bonds; iv. unpaid wages from in-state employers; v. insurance or death benefits payable to the estate; vi. other tangible or intangible personal property; vii. or an unreleased interest in a mortgage on real estate.

Under the out-of-court affidavit approach, a personal representative or heir prepares a statement, usually sworn under oath before a notary, indicating that he/she is entitled to a certain asset that institutions holding properties like a bank account can rely on as sufficient authority to release the asset. The institutions receiving such affidavits are, of course, relieved of all liability in doing so.

To take advantage of the simplified probate approach, a suitable person deemed by the court to have a sufficient interest (e.g. a spouse or next of kin) may file an sworn statement (i.e., an affidavit) with the court stating that all debts of the estate are paid (e.g. to the extent of assets available) and that the aggregate value of the allowed property does not exceed the statutory threshold of $X and/or that the estate holds no real estate. Likely the affidavit must also indicate whether the decedent received aid or care from the state (including a veterans home or hospital commission). This latter requirement would be required so that the court has sufficient time, e.g., 30 days, to give notice to the state, which may have a claim for expenses of care (e.g. Medicaid) provided to the deceased.

After the affidavit is filed, the court can order payment of claims, distribution of the proceeds and transfer of titled property such as automobiles.

NOTE: Even under the small estate procedure, a state succession or transfer tax may still have to be paid, so the affiant must still prepare and file any required tax returns.

File for admission of Will to Probate

Unless the will is submitted to the court without probate, the will is submitted together with an Application for Administration or Probate of Will or similar named form. Note: There is a functionally descriptive list of typical probate forms at end of this Handbook. These or other special forms can usually be obtained at the court clerk's office.

The application will likely contain sworn representations or answers to printed questions about the status of the estate. For example, the "Petitioner" (the proposed fiduciary who makes the application) indicates whether or not there was a will, any divorces or children born after the will was made, etc. All applicable questions must be answered.

Within a certain time, typically 10 days after receipt of the Application for Probate and submission of the Will, the court will publish notice in a local newspaper. The court will set a date for a hearing to establish the validity of the will and appoint the executor or administrator. Also, it will send personal notices to those who would be heirs of the estate under the intestacy laws, i.e. the next of kin, beneficiaries, trustees, charities and others listed on the application form. Everyone should be listed who might, if the will was declared invalid, be in line to inherit the decedent's estate.

Therefore, it is important to include the full names, addresses, zip codes and relationship of all such persons in the application. Minors (with their date of birth) and those in the armed forces should also be included. Also, obtain the Social Security numbers of everyone listed. You will need these numbers later for the estate's tax returns (both income and estate or succession tax returns).

Usually, anyone who is interested in the estate and who objects to the will or to the proposed executor or administrator may attend the hearing. Since proceedings in the Probate Court are often conducted in an informal manner, it may not necessary for the parties to have an attorney with them. (Check with the court clerk.)

However, if a will is likely to be challenged, all the parties would be wise to hire legal counsel to represent them at such hearings. Also, if challenges are made, the court may conduct the hearing on a more formal basis. A court reporter may be requested to transcribe the proceedings to preserve a record for appeals.

Generally, wills are admitted if they are shown to have been properly executed and witnessed (e.g. acknowledged to have been made by the Testator on a voluntary basis while of sound mind and memory, etc.). The actual dispositions directed by a will are not in and of themselves sufficient grounds for having a will declared invalid. Note: marriage, divorce, annulment, or the birth or adoption of children after a will is made may result in the statutory revocation of the will, if it does not provide for such contingencies. Also, a surviving spouse may elect to use for life certain share (typically half or one-third depending on the state) in value of all the property, legally or equitably owned by a deceased spouse. Of course, all distributions are first subject to the prior payment of debts and charges against the estate. Where spouses are entitled to claim against the will, their election to do so must be filed within a certain period, for example, two months after the time for filing of creditors' claims. [See the section on Claims.]

Consult with an attorney if you believe there are grounds for challenging a will.

The court may dispense with a hearing if the will is accompanied by an affidavit in proof of the will and if all entitled parties waive notice of the hearing and have no objection to the granting of the fiduciary letters. This is done by the filing of a form called a General Waiver or similar terminology.

Minors or incompetent persons will have to be represented by guardians ad litem, who will be formally appointed by the court to represent and protect such minors' interests. Such guardians are often required to be independent of other parties involved in settlement of the estate, even the parents of the minors and must be bonded.

Bonding

Regardless of the common provision written into most wills asking the court to dispense with the requirement for a fiduciary bond, the appointed fiduciary should expect to be ordered by the court to post a bond. The amount of bond is a function of the fair estimated value of the estate. Many courts are loath to dispense with the bonding requirement for individuals because they have no knowledge of the proposed fiduciary. They may be more inclined to dispense with the bond if the proposed fiduciary is a large, well known financial institution.

Even if the will states that no bond is required, the court may nonetheless require one. For sizable estates, the court typically requires a bond, since the purpose is to provide funds to indemnify creditors and beneficiaries in the event that estate property is mishandled by the fiduciary.

Note: "Mishandling" an estate implies many things. There may be just general negligence (e.g. failure to pay creditors, file or pay taxes when due, etc.) or more serious problems, such as willful misappropriation of estate assets by the fiduciary. The fiduciary is personally liable for damages or losses resulting from the mishandling of the estate.

A surety is required on every bond. A surety is a person or company (authorized to do business in the state) that the court deems acceptable to ensure that funds will be available to pay any damages or cover losses. A personal surety must reside and have real estate in the state. Surety companies charge annual premiums (based on the size of the estate) for as long as the estate is open and until the bond is released by the court.

The amount of the bond is determined by the size of the estate. It will typically be the greater of (a) twice the decedent's debts, or (b) the amount of estimated succession taxes plus unpaid property taxes, or (c) an amount set by the will.

Notify creditors of any change of address

You will need to collect all of decedent's bills due at death and papers showing any liabilities. Write down the names, addresses and telephone numbers of all likely creditors. You will need such a list in order to send any required formal court notices or payments to creditors.

Giving all creditors prompt notice of decedent's demise is absolutely necessary not only to ensure that all bills are received at an appropriate address (i.e., executor's address), but to begin to put decedent's creditors on notice regarding the requirement that they submit final claims.

OVERVIEW OF ESTATE ADMINISTRATION

Collect the Property of the Decedent

As soon as the executor or administrator is appointed, he or she should conduct a diligent search for and take control of all of the decedent's property.

Personal Items

It is customary for the surviving family to continue to use or keep personal property such as clothing and furnishings that were owned by the decedent. However, these items should be inventoried as soon as possible. Ordinary personal items are usually valued at nominal amounts since they will have little or no market value.

Except for items of little monetary value, personal property should not be transferred without court authorization for partial or final distribution. The actual method of transfer is by simple delivery of the items to those persons entitled thereto under the decedent's will or the intestacy laws.

Automobiles

Automobiles may be used, although the insurance agent should be contacted to ensure continued coverage of surviving drivers. If the estate is probated, the court's consent should be obtained for continued use of vehicles for which title was in the decedent's name only. This may sometimes be done informally, depending on the state, by contacting the court for its permission (the court clerk should notate the file accordingly).

When the vehicle is sold or transferred or needs to be relicensed, a number of documents are typically required by state motor vehicle departments: (a) the fiduciary's certificate of appointment, or a decree in lieu of administration (current, certified copies or a small estate affidavit properly executed); (b) the current registration certificate, indicating that a sale or transfer is being made and to whom; (c) the license plates [which may be retained if requested by family members (parents, siblings, children or spouse)]; (d) assigned certificate of title; (e) a death certificate. If title is lost, it may be necessary to apply first for a duplicate certificate of title.; (f) sales tax form; (g) official application for (new) registration and title certificate.

Note: A sales, use or other transfer tax will likely have to paid for vehicles sold to third parties. However, a transfer made thru the estate to an heir or into the estate's name may not trigger such a tax.

In most states, specific re-titling requirements and filing fees are listed online.

Re-titling instructions for the State of Illinois:
http://www.cyberdriveillinois.com/departments/vehicles/title_registration/corrected_deceased.html.

Jointly owned vehicles (e.g. held in survivorship, as "J. Doe or M. Doe") should be re-titled as soon as possible. Some states, like Illinois, require re-titling within a set period (180 days from date of death in Illinois.) The surviving owner should sign the registration card, indicating "deceased" by the decedent's name or on the appropriate line or box on the form.

If owned in common tenancy (e.g. " J. Doe and M. Doe"), the survivor should sign the reregistration card when received, and have the fiduciary sign the renewal card for the "Estate of ... " the deceased. If the vehicle is then to be transferred solely to the survivor, go through the full reregistration process.

The executor should obtain a dealer's written estimate of the current market value of any automobiles or other vehicles. Also, a copy of the town's personal property assessment should be obtained if one is not found in the decedent's records.

Bank Accounts

At the very least, bank accounts should be transferred into the estate's name. This is readily accomplished by taking a current copy of the executor's letters (as certified by the court) to the bank, together with the bank account numbers (take the statements or books or certificates with you). The bank will prepare new signature cards for the fiduciary to sign.

As a practical matter, especially where the decedent maintained multiple bank accounts, it is easier to close all existing accounts and combine them in a single estate account. The bank should always be given a letter requesting the balance and the amount of any accrued but unpaid interest as of the date of death. This information will be needed to correctly prepare the inventory, the accountings, and the tax returns.

The fiduciary should open a checking account in the name of the estate. This will be needed to keep track of expenses of the estate. The new account's statements and checks are used in accounting for the expenses and other payments of estate funds from the beginning of the estate.

Partial or final distribution of funds in bank accounts should be withheld until the court orders partial or final distribution. The best way to transfer money is by check - the fiduciary should transfer any funds into the estate account, and then write a check to the beneficiary or other person receiving the funds (e.g. a guardian of a minor). This way, a permanent record is kept showing the amount and date of such distributions. However, if the fiduciary wishes to actually transfer a bank account itself, he should prepare and present a certificate of appointment to the bank with a letter of direction.

Safe Deposit Boxes

Once the fiduciary is appointed, safe deposit boxes may be emptied and surrendered by the fiduciary. (See earlier discussion of safe deposit boxes access requirements.)

In probate cases, a representative of the decedent's estate (the appointed executor) will have to bring proper paperwork to the safe deposit company, namely a court authorizing the executor to remove contents (other than a will) from the box.

Securities

The decedent's stock broker or the transfer agents for the decedent's stocks, bonds, mutual funds, and other security accounts should be contacted and requested to send dividend and interest or other payments to the fiduciary. The fiduciary should enclose a current, certified copy of the certificate of appointment with a letter of direction to the agents. The fiduciary's signature on the letter should be guaranteed by a bank, so that the transfer agents can accept the letter as proper authority to make the change.

The fiduciary should ask the agent for a list of final transfer requirements with any special forms that the transfer agent may ultimately require.

However, it is not necessary to have stock or bond certificates transferred into or registered in the estate's name. When the estate is closed, the property can be transferred directly into the beneficiaries' names. At that time, the fiduciary will have to provide the transfer agent with various forms, including IRS W-9 tax identification number for the beneficiaries; a signature-guaranteed letter of direction; the original certificates for the securities (if any); and perhaps a letter of domicile and IRS or state death tax waivers (depending on the agent's requirements).

Real Estate

Within the required period, file a Certificate of Notice for Land Records for all real property owned only by decedent (including decedent's share of property owned with others as tenant in common). The form must be filed with recording or tax office clerk's office for the taxing jurisdiction where real estate is actually located. Giving such notice is necessary to ensure that the tax authority sends the annual tax bill(s) to the personal representative for timely payment of annual real estate taxes. Failure to pay taxes can result in loss of the real estate.

Legal title to real properties that were held in joint tenancy with rights in a named survivor (e.g. the spouse) automatically vests in the surviving joint tenant. However, when the estate is closed (or at the time of sale of titled property), it will be necessary to obtain the court's notice of transfer to be recorded on the town clerk's records.

Naturally, steps should be taken to protect the real property. For example, if a building is vacant, it should be properly insured, weatherized and locked.

To sell real estate (or any other property for that matter) the fiduciary should obtain necessary tax waiver forms from the state or federal tax authorities. Real estate (owned only by decedent) may be formally transferred by court order authorizing the sale and issuance of a fiduciary's deed. The fiduciary must apply to the court for authority to execute sales contracts and executors deeds, unless the fiduciary has such authority, i.e. if the will already directs the real estate sale or gives the fiduciary that power.

Partition of undivided interests in real property

The fiduciary may request the court to partition property owned as tenants in common; the court will decide whether partitioning will serve the best interests of the estate and the interested parties. If partitioning is not feasible, the court may order the real estate to be sold.

Income and "products of" real estate

The fiduciary takes over the management and control of any income producing real estate and has the responsibility to collect rents, harvest crops, etc. Income and the products of real estate (such as crops) vest in the fiduciary as personal property and thus potentially would add to the remainder of the estate (and would thus not belong to those heirs designated to receive specific parcels of real estate), unless otherwise provided for in the decedent's will.

Upon application for partial or final distribution, a court issued document certifying ownership (e.g. Certificate of Ownership) may be issued by the court and should be filed with the clerk of the town where the property is located so that the official change of ownership appears in the land records. Normally, final distribution would not occur until the court has held a hearing on the final accounting and has ordered distribution to the beneficiaries under the will.

For property passing to a joint tenant (with rights of survivorship), the court will not issue a certificate of ownership (since title to the property does not pass by will.). Instead, the court will issue a certificate concerning the payment and release of the estate or succession tax lien, which certificate should then be recorded with the recording clerk on the land records.

Private Business Interests

The fiduciary should apply to the court for permission to continue any business or progress of the business. This may be desirable in order to preserve the value of inventory, products being manufactured, maintain the value of goodwill and dispose of the business or its assets in an orderly manner.

Prepare and File the Inventory

An inventory of the decedent's assets must be filed by the fiduciary typically within two or three months after the acceptance of the bond or other qualification of the fiduciary.

Most courts have discretion for good cause to extend the time for filing the inventory, i.e. for a period measured in most cases from the date of fiduciary's qualification. Certain sales of property (such as real estate) may require the prior filing of the inventory. Property sales likely must be confirmed by the fiduciary filing a verification of sale form with the court.

If the fiduciary fails to file the inventory and appraisals as required, the court may call the fiduciary for an explanation. If the fiduciary had no proper cause for the delay in filing the inventory and does not file immediately, the court must remove the fiduciary.

The inventory should list all the property of the decedent except out of state real estate (which no doubt will be subject to ancillary probate in the state where it is located). The decedent's property must be appraised at fair market value by the fiduciary or by an appraiser chosen by the fiduciary. Debts, such as mortgages on real property, should be listed as part of the property description but netted out of the inventory value.

Any interested party may object to the inventory within a given time (typically 60 days) from the filing of the inventory and appraisal. The court then will order a hearing on whether or not to accept the inventory and appraisal, for example "within 60 days before but not less than 15 or 30 days after the filing of the objections". The fiduciary must make any changes to the inventory and appraisal as the court may require.

Inventory Items on Succession Tax Returns

Few states today have a succession or inheritance type of tax, which is a tax paid by the recipient.

By contrast, a majority do impose a "pass on" estate tax, since Federal law allows a credit for state death taxes paid by an estate. Those that do[1] require filing of a special inheritance or succession tax return within a specified time (for example, "within 9 months from date of death".

An inheritance or succession tax is a tax on transfers of property that occur because of death. (See the definition). Usually, all transferred property is subject to the tax, not just the property shown on the probate inventory.

As a general rule, property transferred by will or intestacy is taxable, as is property transferred by gift or grant (e.g. in trust) which is intended to take effect "in possession or enjoyment" at or after death (such as a remainder interest that passes after a life estate owned by a decedent in certain assets). States that have a succession tax typically include any property that was given while decedent was alive but "in contemplation of" death, typically within 3 years of death. Such state laws presume that all transfers made within 3 years of death were made in contemplation of death. Thus, the tax cannot be avoided by having the deceased make deathbed transfers or gifts within that time, unless it can be proven by the estate that such transfers were not made in contemplation of death. For example, the estate should be able to prove that a bona fide sale of property which was made for fair market value within three years of death was not a taxable transfer for inheritance tax purposes.

Since title to jointly owned property passes because of death, such property is also subject to the inheritance tax - in proportion to the number of joint tenants. For example, if the decedent was one of three joint tenants, $1/3^{rd}$ of the value of the joint property would be included as taxable property in the inheritance tax return.

Note: Transfers in contemplation of death or if use or enjoyment is retained by decedent may be subject to full taxation, even where property is held in joint tenancy.

Succession tax returns usually must be filed in duplicate with the Probate Court, which has the responsibility to send a copy to the state tax authority.

If the court is of the opinion that the estate is not subject to succession or inheritance taxes, the court must notify the state revenue (tax) department of that fact, and send up any tax returns that have been filed. The tax commissioner then has a given time (e.g. 60 days) to object. If there is no objection to the

---

[1] The rate may be fixed or may depend on who inherits the property. Indiana, Iowa, Kentucky, Maryland, Nebraska, New Jersey, Pennsylvania and Tennessee have succession taxes.

court's certificate of no tax, then the estate is free from such taxes, unless the appraised value of any item on the return is increased or property worth more than a threshold amount ($X) is newly discovered.

Note: It is beyond the scope of this handbook to discuss death taxes in depth. It should be mentioned, however, that the fiduciary may have a duty to file a Federal Estate Tax return (form 706) if the decedent's estate (including certain lifetime gifts) exceeds the Unified Credit equivalent in value.

Also, if a Federal Estate Tax return has to be filed, states levying an estate tax will require filing of a state Estate Tax return where a Federal estate tax is payable to the IRS and a state estate tax credit is taken by the estate.

The fiduciary must also be concerned with filing the decedent's last individual tax return (IRS form 1040), and income tax returns (IRS form 1041) for the estate (for each tax year that the estate is open). State income tax returns for the estate may also have to be filed.

A list of federal tax forms and state death tax forms (under more functional names) is included at the end of this book.

Settle Decedent's Debts or Claims Against the Estate

Debts and claims against the estate should be paid before distributions are made to the beneficiaries. It is critically important that the fiduciary quickly move to discover outstanding claims of the decedent and then to initiate the process for cutting off all known claims as soon as possible by properly notifying known creditors, listing and evaluating the submitted claims, denying those thought to be invalid, and then filing such claims as required with the Probate Court so as to trigger the claims cut-off dates.

However, if creditors do not properly file or "exhibit" their claims (i.e. notify the fiduciary of their claims), they risk having the claims denied.

Claims are paid according to priorities: (1) funeral expenses; (2) estate administration expenses; (3) costs of decedent's last illness; (4) federal or state taxes and associated claims (interest, penalties); (5) workers or mechanics (tradesmen's) claims for services rendered; (6) other preferred claims; (7) all other claims (proportioned among them).

As a practical matter, ordinary creditors should be notified by the fiduciary of any billing change of address, e.g. to be sent to the fiduciary's address.

The court must, within a specified time (typically 2 weeks or 14 days) after appointment of the first fiduciary, publish notice of probate in the local newspapers. This notice gives the estate's (decedent's) name, and the fiduciary's name and address. It then states that claimants should promptly present their claims to the fiduciary, or risk losing their rights on the claim. Special notice is given to the state veterans home and hospital commission if applicable.

Usually, the Probate Court will order the fiduciary to give "Notice to Creditors to Present Claims" in writing, certified mail, return receipt requested. Creditors receiving such notice usually have 90 days or more to present their claims. The fiduciary has to review the court's file after the claims filing deadline to make a note of any creditors' names submitted by beneficiaries or by creditors directly to the court.

Creditors not so notified (i.e., those having only the benefit of the published news notice) have only until the statutory cut-off date of appointment of the first fiduciary to present their claims. Ordinarily, failure to do so before the fiduciary distributes assets to beneficiaries will discharge the fiduciary from liability. However, the fiduciary may still be liable if he fails to notify a creditor when he actually knows of a claim or if he has been asked by a beneficiary to notify the creditor. In those cases, the fiduciary has another X days to file his "Return and List of Claims" with the court.

The fiduciary may take the initiative to cut off claims, by sending proper notice (fiduciary's name, address, estate name, etc.) to known creditors. If a creditor fails to present his claim within the specified time, again typically 90 days from the date of the notice, then the creditor may not recover on the claim.

Beneficiaries may force the fiduciary to give such notice by providing the court with creditors' names and addresses. The court will within statutory time thereafter, certify a list of potential claimants. It is the fiduciary's responsibility to get the list from the court.

Many states have a fall-back for creditors who have failed, through no fault of their own, to present claims within the specified period; such creditors may apply for an extension within a set time from the date of the fiduciary's notice. The fiduciary can demand that claimants properly prove all claims with proper evidence.

The claimant must give due creditor offsets for all prior payments and account for security held. Claims must be made in accordance with the law, e.g. by delivery or registered mail postage prepaid, sent to the court or the fiduciary.

The fiduciary must notify claimants of any rejection (in whole or in part) of their claims [It is a good idea to mail notice of allowance or disallowance to creditors or claimants by registered mail, return receipt requested}. If a claim is not paid or rejected within 90 days from the date of presentation, then the claimant may give notice to the fiduciary to act on the claim. If the fiduciary fails to act within 30 days from such notice, the claim is treated as rejected.

No claimant may institute a suit to collect the claim until the claim is rejected. Then, he has a certain statutory period from the date of rejection to file a suit, or X days from the date of rejection to ask the Probate Court to hear and decide upon the claim. The court may hear the case, or in some states even appoint a commission of one or more disinterested persons to decide the claim.

Even though creditors may have no rights against the estate (or fiduciary), beneficiaries may still be liable for the payment of administrative expenses, taxes, funeral expenses or other claims, up to the extent of the value of the property they have received from the estate.

The fiduciary is not responsible for paying off secured creditors out of the general (residuary) estate, unless the will "expressly or by necessary implication" states otherwise. A will generally directing the fiduciary to pay the debts of the estate is not to be taken as a clear indication that such secured debts are to be paid off by the estate before distribution. Therefore, unpaid mortgages on real estate (or secured liens against other property) may go with the subject property upon distribution. In such circumstances, mortgage holders or other security holders may foreclose on the subject property if the mortgage or other lien is not paid. Beneficiaries receiving such property are liable up to the extent of the value of the property that they have received.

Claims against insolvent estates: If the fiduciary cannot reach a settlement with all creditors of the estate, he should petition the Probate Court to implement the statutory settlement process. Unless the estate has very little in the way of assets, the court may decide the validity of the claim or appoint a commission of independent persons to hear and decide upon claims against an insolvent estate. Claimants are paid based on the priority of their claim and in proportion to the amount of their claim to the assets available. Except on government claims or for funeral or last illness expenses, suits may not be filed against an insolvent estate, nor may judgments against the decedent (received prior to death) be fulfilled ("executed") by a law officer's (e.g. a sheriff's) seizure of property.

Because of the complexity of the law, fiduciaries facing large amounts of claims, or contested claims or large but insolvent estates should, for the fiduciary's protection, obtain professional advice as to proper claims procedures.

After the allowed statutory claims-filing period expires, the fiduciary should file the Return Notice and List of Claims with the court. This form should show all claims that the fiduciary has allowed or disallowed. Barring any otherwise valid claims being filed, the fiduciary should now be in a position to prepare to close the estate.

Account for the Fiduciary's Administration of the Estate

During the administration of the estate, the fiduciary will have received income and paid the death taxes and claims against the estate, as well as expenses arising out of the administration of the estate.

The nominal time for administration of a well run estate is 12 months. Depending upon the will, the estate may have received interest that is payable to the beneficiaries who are entitled to specific bequests of money or personal property (e.g. stocks or bonds), or to the income produced by specifically devised real estate.

However, it seldom happens that an estate (a large one at any rate) can be closed within the first year. One of the reasons is that the federal and state tax authorities are usually slow to review the death tax returns, and it may be necessary for the fiduciary to appear in audit proceedings before the tax authorities in order to negotiate and finally settle the death taxes due.

The fiduciary may therefore have to prepare an interim accounting for submission to the court. The fiduciary should determine whether partial distributions of assets or payments of net estate income should be made to the entitled beneficiaries.

In any event, a final accounting must usually be prepared and submitted to the court for approval before the estate is closed. It is usual to request the court's permission to distribute all remaining assets in accordance with the will, or the intestate succession laws, when the final accounting is submitted.

The basic purposes of accountings are: (1) to disclose to the court that the fiduciary has properly handled the estate's finances; (2) to show the receipt and application of all income and payment of allowable expenses; and (3) to show the various transactions concerning the assets of the estate (e.g. liquidating sales and distributions of assets). The beneficiaries naturally have a right to review the accounts to determine how much they will receive from the estate. After receipt, the court will give them reasonable notice of a hearing to file any objections concerning the accounts of the fiduciary.

If, except for specific bequests, the fiduciary is the sole beneficiary of the estate or all beneficiaries are also fiduciaries, it may not be necessary to file an accounting. Instead, they can file a Statement in Lieu of Account. The fiduciaries must state under oath that all expenses, debts and taxes are paid and list all claims returned. The court may then discharge the fiduciaries and release any bond.

Prepare and File Income Tax Returns

Another reason for maintaining the accounts of the estate is that the fiduciary usually must file income tax returns for the estate to report income received during administration, e.g. IRS form 1041 returns and state income tax returns.

Note: the fiduciary is also responsible for filing the decedent's last 1040 for the tax year ending with the date of death. The fiduciary may file a joint return with a surviving spouse, or elect to file a separate return for the deceased. Likewise, if a trust or trusts are associated with the estate, it may be necessary to file income tax returns declaring any taxable income earned by such trust(s) during the estate settlement period.

Regular accounts should be kept in order to prepare proper income tax returns for the estate. Fiduciaries must file income tax returns for any year in which the estate had $600 or more of gross income or where a beneficiary of the estate is a foreign national. A state income tax return will likely also have to be filed if taxable income exceeds a certain minimum. It may be desirable for the fiduciary to make partial distributions (with the court's approval) to income beneficiaries before the end of the tax year, e.g. if the beneficiaries are in a lower tax bracket than the estate. Usually, the estate will be allowed a deduction for distributed income.

Note that estate income tax rates in 2010 increase from 15% to 35% when income taxable to the estate exceeds $11,200.

The fiduciary may elect a tax year ending the last day of any calendar month, through the 11 the month after the date of death.

For example, if a decedent died on 12/31/11, the 1st tax year of the estate would end 1/1/12, unless the fiduciary elected to end the first tax year at the end of an earlier month.

Note: Detailed discussion of income, estate, inheritance and succession taxes is beyond the scope of this publication. Needless to say, the non-professional fiduciary should consult with a qualified tax expert in such cases.

Distribute Assets and File the Closing Statement

Now it is time for the fiduciary to review the estate to ensure that:

(a) all allowed claims and taxes have been paid (and tax lien waivers filed);

(b) final income tax returns have been filed (and any taxes payable by the estate have been paid);

(c) the final account has been approved by the court;

(d) the assets are properly distributed by court order (e.g. per will or under intestacy law);

(e) any survivorship tax certificates (for jointly held real estate) have been recorded on the land records;

(f) an application to surrender possession of other real estate has been approved (and the Certificate of Devise has been recorded);

(g) any applications for refund of death tax overpayments have been filed;

(h) application for appointment of any testamentary trustee (for a trust created under the will) has been approved.

The fiduciary should obtain signed receipts from all beneficiaries (or their duly appointed guardian) for any distributions.

Then, the fiduciary should file the appropriate court document needed to formally close the estate, e.g., an Affidavit of Closing of Decedent's Estate. This being done, the fiduciary should obtain the court's certificate for release of any probate bond. The certificate should be sent to the surety company by the fiduciary (if the court has not already done so) to secure the release of the bond. For most practical-purposes, probate administration is then ended. After one year, the court will send notice that its file of papers may be picked up by the fiduciary, or they will be destroyed.

The estate, if properly handled, should not be subject to reopening, although there may be collateral issues such as delayed estate income tax audits, or suits on disputed claims distributions to beneficiaries.

_____

PROBATE FORMS, CHECKLISTS & OTHER STEPS

Birth Certificate

If necessary get a copy from the vital statistics department at the local government office where decedent was born.

Death Certificate

Ask the funeral director for at least 10 copies to begin with. The death certificate will show decedent's domicile at death, place of death, date of death, time of death, cause of death, duration of last illness. I will also show attending physician and his address. You will need this information in preparing papers for the Probate Court and to prepare death tax returns.

Immediate information required

Information about the Decedent

Legal Name:			
Aliases Used:			
Name on Will:			
Father's Name			
Mother's Name:			
Place of Birth:			
Birthdate:			
Sex:	**Age**:	**Race**:	**Married**:
Spouse's Name/Address:			
Widowed:	**Divorced**:	(Former Spouse Name/Address)	
Decedent's Date of Death:			
Duration of Last Illness:			
Place of Death (City, County State):			
Permanent Residence Address (Domicile):			
Social Security Number:			

Occupation: Veteran: Yes   No
Which War(s):   Which Service:
Name/Address of Person providing information:
Did decedent receive any public assistance or state hospital or health care, and if so, what type (e.g. Title 19 Medicaid support) from what agency:

Burial Information

Name of Funeral Director: Telephone:
Address:
Place of Burial:
Memorial Headstone/Other ordered from:
No. of Certified Death Certificates Requested from Director:

Will Information

Located where?
Will Dated: Proof of Will Affidavit: Yes   No
Codicils to Will Dated: After last will or codicil?
Subsequent: remarriage?   birth of child?   or divorce?
Details [Dates, to whom, where, termination dates, type of situation]:

Gifts in Contemplation of Death

Did the Decedent make any gifts within 3 years prior to death? If so, specify what was given, the value of the gifts made (at the time of the gifts), the person receiving the gift and why the gift was made (e.g. education, medical expense, other) and if gift tax returns were filed (get copies):
Date of Entry to Decedent's last residence:
Who was present?:
Note: list additional information about gifts on separate sheet

DETERMINE HEIRS OF THE ESTATE

Heirs are determined either (a) according the state's intestacy law if there is no will, or (b) according to who was named a beneficiary to receive what asset under decedent's will. If heirs are in doubt, the laws of intestacy will apply. List the names and addresses (with zip codes) and relationship of all known heirs, next of kin, beneficiaries, and trustees of the estate:

List immediate heirs first

Surviving spouse, children, parents of Testator, grandchildren (especially survivors of a deceased child of Testator).

List secondary heirs

Brothers & sisters, their children (if parent deceased), uncles & aunts. first cousins, then second cousins, etc.

List other heirs

All others named in will or entitled by laws of intestacy.

1. Name: Address: SS#:
2. Name: Address: SS#:
3. Name: Address: SS#:
4. Name: Address: SS#:
5. Name: Address: SS#:
6. Name: Address: SS#:

7. Name:
Address:
SS#:

8. Name:
Address:
SS#:

9. Name:
Address:
SS#:

10. Name:
Address:
SS#:

11. Name:
Address:
SS#:

12. Name:
Address:
SS#:

13. Name:
Address:
SS#:

14. Name:
Address:
SS#:

ESTIMATE THE SIZE OF THE ESTATE

Use information gathered on lists following, i.e., for Assets and Claims .

First, add up all assets

ASSETS	$ VALUE (Aggregate)	SUBTOTAL
PERSONAL PROPERTY held in name of Decedent		
Bank Accounts		
Securities		
Private Businesses		
Valuable Personal Property		
Death Benefits		
Automobiles / Other Vehicles		
Personal Items and Furniture		
Social Security / Veterans Benefits		
Subtotal of "Personal Property" →		
REAL ESTATE →		
Total of ASSETS →	→	→

Next, total & deduct all liabilities

LIABILITIES		
Regular Bills (home, auto, insurance, utilities, etc.)		
Medical		
Personal Loans (include credit cards)		
Mortgages		
Unpaid Taxes (Property, Income – Fed. & State)		
Funeral Expenses		
Total LIABILITIES →		
*Plus Estimated Probate Administration Costs		
Total Estimated Tax Deductions →		
Assets – Deductions = Estimated Taxable Assets → (i.e., Bondable Estate ~ 5%)	→	

Ancillary Probate

List Assets that are located or subject to probate in another state, and start ancillary probate proceedings in that state (probate jurisdiction): {what, where, value}

ASSETS	$ VALUE
Personal Property	
Real Estate	
Other	

COLLECT ASSET INFORMATION

See Estimating Size of Estate form at earlier page of this Handbook.

List <u>all</u> property in which Decedent's had an interest

Identify different <u>legal</u> kinds of property

Properties, especially real estate, are commonly classified as follows: <u>joint ownership</u> with rights of survivor (i.e., Joint Tenancy or JTWROS); <u>tenancy in common</u> (titleholders own an undivided portion of property, e.g. 50/50); and <u>solely owned</u> (decedent was 100% titleholder). For death tax purposes, a fourth category may be important, namely, property gifted "in contemplation of death".

Even though Decedent held an interest in joint property before death, such property is usually <u>not</u> subject to probate. However, property held jointly may be subject to death taxes (e.g., the Federal estate tax). And decedent's will may distribute property to different heirs based on a classification, i.e., "I give all my shares of real estate held as tenant-in-common to my son, John Jones".

It is therefore important to begin listing all of decedent's assets by including these classifications and full property descriptions as well as the date of death values of all properties (joint and other) in which Decedent had an interest at the time of death. The values of the different classes of property can then be separated from each other for probate, tax and estate distribution purposes.

Bank Accounts

List all account information, i.e., Name, Account #, Type of Account {savings, checking, CD, IRA or other retirement accounts}, $ balance at date of death, amount of accrued interest due on date of death. Names on accounts, i.e. in the name of joint tenants with rights of survivorship, or in decedent's name only?

Securities

List name of and type of security {publicly listed company stocks - preferred or common; or corporate or government bonds, mutual funds, options, calls, puts, brokers margin accounts, and related rights}, series or bond numbers, face value of bonds, number of shares, value on date of death, amount of dividends declared but unpaid or accrued interest owed as of date of death)

Private Businesses

List name and location of business and type (i.e. corporation, partnership), value of stock (if a corporation), or value of payout from buy-sell agreement, or net worth value of decedent's interest in the business on the date of death. Also, royalties, accounts receivable, and similar items owed to decedent on date of death.

Valuable Personal Property

Describe decedent's jewelry, coin or stamp or other collections, artwork, antiques; appraised value on date of death.

Life Insurance

Life insurance owned by Decedent on his/her own life should be included in the Probate Estate, if it is payable to the estate (check the beneficiary designation on the policy.)

If life insurance is payable to another person, trust, or other beneficiary, it is not part of the Probate Estate but may be subject to estate or inheritance taxes so that determination will have to be made by the executor or personal representative of the estate.

Life insurance held in a trust no part of the proceeds of which are payable to Decedent's estate should not be included in the Probate Estate. Most insurance companies have payout department that will be helpful and happy to answer questions about how to cash out their policies and finalize arrangements for payment. Contact them as soon as possible after Decedent's death – most companies issue policy payout checks quickly and the cash can be very useful to help support beneficiaries, if not the estate itself.

Death Benefits

Company paid insurance and fraternal societies benefits

List benefits payable to estate - insurance company name, policy number, type of policy (whole, term), face value of policy, amount of loans against value, accrued dividends and interest due before or from date of death.

Retirement plan benefits

List all of Decedent's IRA's, pension, profit sharing and 401 k, etc., that are payable to Decedent's estate or that are contribution-based values (e.g. company paid based on Decedent's earnings) and payable to named beneficiaries.

Social Security and Veterans Benefits

Type, amount payable and to whom.

Automobiles/Other Vehicles

Boats, airplanes, etc. Need title certificates & license registrations; appraised values on date of death.

Personal Belongings

Clothing, personal effects, furnishings, etc. Need descriptions and date of death appraised values.

Real Estate

Address of, legal description (per deed), percentage or type of interest (i.e. sole owner, tenant in common or joint tenant with rights of survivorship, market value on date of death, taxes due and assessed value (see last tax bill).

Valuable artwork, antiques, collections, etc.

One reason that the executor or personal representative of the estate needs to move fast to secure and preserve Decedent's assets is that valuables like this may be regarded by certain heirs as "their" property immediately upon Decedent's death. Under the law, they may have a valid beneficial claim to such property, but are NOT entitled to take possession of such assets unless and until authorized to do so in accordance with an *order of distribution* issued by the Probate Court.

The executor/representative of the estate can be held to be personally liable for any asset losses, estate and transfer taxes, claims against the estate, etc. after he/she/it has been officially appointed by the court or else has as a practical matter already taken control of the Decedent's assets. Obviously, therefore it is important to warn (nicely) the apparent heirs of the executor/representative's responsibilities in looking after their interests in the estate and that they will be held responsible for any of Decedent's property in their possession or under their control.

Estimate the date of death values if necessary and add them up.

LIST ALL KNOWN DEBTS AND CLAIMS

Regular Bills

Include all household bills due and payable on date of death; Medical: Doctors, hospital, laboratory and pharmacy expenses: unpaid before or at time of death.

Personal Loans

List lenders' names and addresses, account numbers, balances due and accrued interest due on all credit cards, personal notes, personal bank loans (not secured by property), secured personal loans, e.g. loans secured by personal property, such as automobiles or stock margin loans].

Mortgages Due

List the name of mortgage lenders and their addresses, account numbers, dates of mortgages and notes (including any revisions); interest rates, payment terms (monthly, annually, etc.), amounts of unpaid loan principal and amount of interest payments remaining unpaid on date of death, as well as relevant details of all real estate encumbered by mortgages.

Unpaid Taxes

Estimate the Federal and state and local income taxes due and unpaid as of date of death; personal property taxes (e.g. auto) assessed and unpaid as of date of death; real estate taxes assessed and unpaid as of date of death;

Funeral Charges

Include all costs of a funeral home or crematorium, flowers, reception, funeral transportation, place of interment, gravestone or other monument.

Estate administration charges

These would include court fees, the cost of a probate bond, executor(s) fees, legal and accounting fees, insurance to protect assets until distribution, costs of transportation incurred in connection with probate, utility and service costs incurred in connection with estate administration, asset distribution costs (e.g. shipping to heirs), and potentially a fair number of other expenses directly related to the probate process. Rule of thumb: use 5% of probate assets to estimate such costs.

Calculate the estimated value of the probate estate

A. Subtract from the total value of <u>all</u> assets the estimated value of jointly held property as well as the value of any tenant-in-common property interests or shares <u>not</u> owned by Decedent (i.e., real estate, automobiles, etc.). Also, be sure to subtract (or not count) any amounts for life insurance proceeds, retirement funds, death benefits unless they are payable to the estate.

The remaining $ value should be referred to as the Probate Estate or by a similar name to distinguish it from the Taxable Estate for death tax purposes and from the Distributable Estate for assets distribution purposes as set forth in the Decedent's will.

B. Use the value of the Probate Estate to fill in the Probate Court's Application for Administration or Probate of Will (or similarly named form).

C. Multiply the Probate Estate by 5% to estimate the estate's Administrative Costs. to the total of estimated debts and expenses.

D. Deduct the Administrative Costs and estimated of Estate Taxes* from the value of the Probate Estate as calculated in A above. The remainder give the estimated value of the Distributable Estate.

E. It may be necessary to determine the value of the Taxable Estate if the estate is a large one. It is recommended that the executor seek advice about this from a qualified professional (e.g., attorney or accountant).

---

*Determining whether any estate taxes will be owed depends upon the size of Decedent's estate and can involve complicated calculations. It goes beyond the scope of this book, as you can see based on what the IRS says about the Federal Estate Tax and how it is determined:

The Estate Tax is a tax on your right to transfer property at your death. It consists of an accounting of everything you own or have certain interests in at the date of death (Refer to Form 706 (PDF)). The fair market value of these items is used, not necessarily what you paid for them or what their values were when you acquired them. The total of all of these items is your "Gross Estate." The includible property may consist of cash and securities, real estate, insurance, trusts, annuities, business interests and other assets.

Once you have accounted for the Gross Estate, certain deductions (and in special circumstances, reductions to value) are allowed in arriving at your "Taxable Estate." These deductions may include mortgages and other debts, estate administration expenses, property that passes to surviving spouses and qualified charities. The value of some operating business interests or farms may be reduced for estates that qualify.

After the net amount is computed, the value of lifetime taxable gifts (beginning with gifts made in 1977) is added to this number and the tax is computed. The tax is then reduced by the available unified credit. Presently, the amount of this credit reduces the computed tax so that only total taxable estates and lifetime gifts that exceed $1,000,000 will actually have to pay tax. In its current form, the estate tax only affects the wealthiest 2 percent of all Americans.

Most relatively simple estates (cash, publicly traded securities, small amounts of other easily valued assets, and no special deductions or elections, or jointly held property) do not require the filing of an estate tax return. A filing is required for estates with combined gross assets and prior taxable gifts exceeding $1,500,000 in 2004 - 2005; $2,000,000 in 2006 - 2008; $3,500,000 for decedents dying in 2009; and $5,000,000 or more for decedent's dying in 2010 or later (note: there are special rules for decedents dying in 2010.

Sourced 6/21/11: http://www.irs.gov/businesses/small/article/0,,id=164871,00.html.

CLAIMS AND DEBTS LIST

Debts and claims against the estate include common bills due at the time of death, costs incurred as a result of death, outstanding loans and mortgages, legal claims (lawsuits), and costs of estate administration.

BILLS:	$ Amount
Utility	
Automotive	
Taxes	
Insurance	
Housing	
Food	
Medical	
Other	
LOANS & MORTGAGES	
LAWSUITS	
COSTS OF ESTATE ADMINISTRATION	

STEPS AFTER APPOINTMENT OF FIDUCIARY

Determine Family or Spouse's Need for Allowance

If the survivors of the deceased need funds for support during probate, obtain and complete form PC 202 Application and Decree for Support Allowance.

Figure how much will be needed monthly and during the first year by the spouse or family for these necessities and use in completing:

Type of Expense	Mo. $ Amount
Food:	
Clothing:	
RX:	
Doctors:	
Dentists:	
Heating:	
Electricity:	
Telephone:	
Home:	
Mortgage Payments:	
Insurance (if not included in mortgage payment):	
Real Estate Taxes (if not included in mortgage payment)	
Health Insurance:	
Life Insurance:	
Education tuition etc 1:	
Child Care:	
Other:	
Total of Monthly Expenses	$
Insert number of months needed (12 months max.) Then multiply by Total of Monthly Expenses above	
TOTAL ALLOWANCE NEEDED	$

NOTE: In order for the court to award an allowance, the fiduciary may have to prepare and file a preliminary inventory for the estate. Also, when determining the need for allowance, make the first estimate of the estate's cash needs, to pay claims, taxes, legacies, etc.

Next Administrative Steps ✓

Notify all likely beneficiaries under the Will (or by intestacy) of their potential interests, They may review the will at the Probate Court, but the fiduciary should, to save the court's time, provide them with a photocopy of the will).	
Notify any charities of potential gifts under the Will.	
Notify all private corporations or partnerships of any interests that were held by deceased (e.g. stock, bonds, buy -sell agreements, pension plans, etc.).	
Notify the state (if it has a claim, as for public health expenses incurred on behalf of the deceased).	
Notify the Veterans Administration and apply for potential death benefits.	
Notify the Social Security Administration and apply for potential death benefits.	
Notify the Post Office of new mailing address e.g. of fiduciary, or post office box.	
Prepare and file an IRS SS-4 identification number application form to obtain an estate Federal tax EID# [You will need this to file estate income tax returns.].	
Prepare and file an IRS Form 56 Notice Concerning Fiduciary Relationship[This will notify the IRS as to the fiduciary's authority to act for the estate, and to send notices, refunds, etc. to the fiduciary.].	

Record "Death Notices" within ____ months from the date of appointment of the fiduciary on the land records in each town where decedent owned real estate. Do this as soon as possible. The certificate of the fiduciary must state the fact and date of death, the decedent's name, his last residence, and whether he left a will.	
Apply to the court for permission to distribute household or personal effects to the immediate family, or sell unwanted items.	
Collect copies of prior income & gift tax returns	
Retain appraisers for tangible and for real property.	
Note: you may have to provide the tax authorities with formal appraisals for valuable property, particularly real estate, in order to prove the fair market values upon which the death tax returns are based.	
Notify insurance companies of the decedent's death and submit policy claims:	
1. Homeowner's (fire, theft, damage):	
2. Public liability (umbrella type):	
3. Auto liability & damage:	
4. Life:	
5. Others:	
Notify financial institutions of fiduciary's appointment, i.e., banks, stock brokers, mutual funds, REITS, etc.	
1. Arrange to transfer accounts to estate's name	
2. Specify where they should to send future statements and 1099 IRS forms	
3. Open estate account and liquidate other accounts & transfer to estate account.	
Note: waivers from tax authorities may be needed in order to transfer accounts, liquidate securities or transfer real estate. Consult with attorney and/or Probate Court as to need to obtain prior court approval to liquidate and/or sell assets.	

Apply for town property tax exemption for widow, minor or parent of (deceased) veteran.	
Establish any necessary ancillary probate in other states where decedent owned property.	
File a wrongful death claim on behalf of estate, if applicable. Note: Contact an attorney for proper advice about this important matter, e.g. if decedent was killed in an accident.	
Determine whether legacies are or may be disclaimed i.e., whether it would be beneficial for surviving spouse or other heirs to disclaim under the will or for tax purposes. Note: the fiduciary may find it necessary or desirable to take action with regard to these matters, particularly if there are parties acting against the interests of the estate (e.g. a surviving spouse is electing against a will) or if the estate could save on death taxes by making certain disclaimer elections. Consult with an attorney for proper advice about this important matter!	

* Date of Death ("DOD"): (for measuring other deadlines) »
* _____ the day from DOD for filing of Will »
* Date of Appointment of Fiduciary »
* Date notice to creditors is published in public news »
* Mail written notices return receipt requested to known creditors to limit their time to file claims »
* Creditors claims date »
* Date to file Inventory with court »
* Date to file Return Notice and List of Claims with court (i.e. showing all claims, whether allowed or disallowed by the fiduciary) »
Tax filing & other important dates:
* Federal estate tax return IRS Form 706 (9 months after DOD) »
* State estate and succession tax return (____ months after DOD) »
Note: If the returns are not finished for filing by such date, apply for an extension and pay the estimated tax due with the extension.
* Decedent's final income tax return (due April 15th in year after DOD) »
* First income tax return for Estate (IRS Form 1041) »

Note: Estate's 1st year begins with DOD and ends with either the last day of 11th month after DOD, or an earlier estate fiscal year to be elected by fiduciary. Also, remember to make any required quarterly estimated payments during estate's taxable year. If the estate continues for more than one year, remember to file returns and pay income taxes due on estate income for each tax year of the estate. Note: There are many tax elections that may be made for an estate. Consult with an qualified attorney or a accountant on all tax issues!

Other Actions Required During Administration of Estate ✓

Determine the desirability of paying pecuniary (money) legacies since interest on legacies is usually payable after the 1st year. First, remember to withhold any amount of taxes if payable out of legacies. Get SS #'s of beneficiaries and their addresses.	
Apply to the court to extend the time for distribution if estate administration is likely to continue past the first year.	
Renew bond (pay premium) if estate extends past 1st year.	
First year or final accounting:	
a. Prepare account	
b. Submit to court with request for order of distribution for any property that should be distributed.	
c. Verify and/or send notices of court hearing on account to all interested beneficiaries (including guardians ad litem for minors or incompetent persons.)	
Note: If the fiduciary is the sole beneficiary (except for specific bequests), consider filing only a Statement in Lieu of Account. On granting the approval of the account the court will file the appropriate public notices to limit the appeal period.	

File death tax payment receipts and property tax receipts with the court. These are required before final account is approved.	
Seek qualification of any trustee named under the will (e.g. a testamentary trustee) with the Probate Court. The trustee may be required to post bond, and either the probate judge or the Secretary of State must be appointed to receive process on behalf of any out-of-state trustee.	
a. Get trustees Acceptance of Trust.	
b. Request court to issue decree approving trustee.	
Note: Trustee must file an initial inventory of trust assets within two months from decree date and file periodic accountings as required by the court.	
Note: If decedent creates an inter vivos trust, the fiduciary may distribute to the trustee of that trust. That trustee must behave in accordance with the trust instrument, but is not usually subject to court supervision except at a beneficiary's request.	
Notify beneficiaries (especially if out-of-state) of the court's approval accounting and order of distribution. Also, send them a copy of the decree, postage prepaid, return receipt requested.	
Note: This will limit the time for any appeal by any beneficiaries. The normal appeal time, if notice is given, is _____ month. Otherwise, in the absence of notice, the statutory appeal time is _____ months.	
Reserve any amount needed to pay disputed or unpaid claims or taxes e.g., death or income taxes, esp. pending any audit and settlement of death taxes.	
Note: Reserves may usually be withheld with the court's approval, which should be requested when submitting the final account and prior to the issuance for the order of distribution)	

Final Tax Returns:	
a. Prepare and file any supplemental succession tax return (e.g. if there is a refund of other taxes by the IRS or other states).	
b. Prepare and file a final Estate Income Tax Return (Form 1041), as well as any state income tax return due. Pay any taxes on or before the time for filing (regardless of any extensions requested.)	
File Certificate of Tax Payment for any joint real property. Note: The court will issue this certificate after state succession taxes are paid, or if. a release of the state's tax lien is issued (and the court is given a copy).	

BASIC PROBATE ACCOUNTING SCHEDULE

You will need to know the following in order to prepare the basic accounting:

Assets & Income Received By Fiduciary

	$ AMOUNT
Inventory as on file	
Additional real/personal property	
Income received	
Dividends	
Interest	
Other	
Total	

Payments & Distributions By Fiduciary

	$ AMOUNT
Claims paid	
Funeral expenses	
Administration expenses	
Legal notices	
Succession Taxes	
Estate Taxes	
Property Taxes (real and personal)	
Probate Court costs	
Fiduciary's fees	
Attorney's fees	
Other disbursements	
Amount on hand for distribution	
Real property	
Personal property	
Total	

Allocation Schedule - Proposed Distributions To	
Names	**Item / $ Value**

SECURITIES TRANSFER - DOCUMENT CHECKLIST

NAME OF SECURITY

_____

☐ Original certificate(e.g. the actual stock or bond or mutual fund share certificate)

☐ Tax transfer form (IRS form W-9):

☐ Current Certificate of Fiduciary Appointment(e.g. no older 0 than 60 days since certification by court):

☐ A Certificate of Decedent's Domicile:0

☐ The fiduciary's letter of direction to the transfer agent to change of name of owner of security, or to sell, and where to send new certificate, dividends, etc.

☐ A signed stock power:(or the fiduciary's proper endorsement of 0 the security on the back, as required by the transfer agent)

☐ Any other documents required by the transfer agent:

NAME OF TRANSFER CONTACT:

_____

TRANSFER AGENT'S NAME & ADDRESS:

_____

TELEPHONE:

_____

DATE CALLED:

_____

TIME CALLED: _____ DATE SECURITY MAILED: _____

DELIVERED BY:

_____

REAL ESTATE TRANSFER - CHECKLIST

PROPERTY (Description/Address:

_____

_____

Decedent's Owner Interest: JTWROS   Tenant in Common   Sole Owner)   Other:

_____

Type of Property: Residential   Commercial   Decedent's   Residence   Rental

Task	✓
For distributions, apply to the Probate Court for certificate of devise:	
For Sale or Other Transfers:	
(a.) apply for court order permitting sale or other transfer of real property and certificate concerning succession taxes.	
(b.) Apply for "Certificate of release offline" on property from state tax authorities (e.g. for property to be sold):	
i. Write letter to state tax authority [Department of Revenue Service] stating the circumstances of sale or transfer (e.g. property being sold to raise funds to pay taxes). Attach copy of property description (including street address and legal description).	
Request release certificate and give return address. Enclose check to cover fee (if any).	
ii. Upon receipt of certificate from the state, file a copy with the court for its information. Also, deliver the certificate to the transferee when delivering the property deed.	
(c.) Apply for federal "Certificate Discharging Property Subject to Estate Tax Lien".	
i. Obtain IRS Form 4422. Fill out completely.	
ii. Attach copy of property address and legal descript- non.	
iii. Send with letter requesting issuance of certificate and address of fiduciary.	
iv. Deliver the certificate to the transferee when delivering the property deed.	
File the court's certificate	
of devise or concerning taxes and with the clerk in town where property is located. Note: the court may do this directly - but check to see exactly when it is filed for the record.	

TAX TIPS

The personal representative or executor (referred to hereafter as the "administrator") of an estate is responsible (and liable) for filing any required local, state and Federal tax returns and for paying taxes due (or collecting refunds on behalf of the estate).

The following list of tax forms is fairly inclusive, but may not reflect changes in tax forms, form names and/or numbers since tax authorities are continually revising their forms to keep pace with new tax legislation.

Administrators of estates need to familiarize themselves with the following tax information:
1. The name and number of the most important tax forms;
2. When tax returns have to be filed.
3. How the filing date may be extended
4. How and when taxes have to be paid

The administrator should remember to apply for a separate tax number from the respective tax authorities as soon as possible after taking over as executor or personal representative. This can usually be done online (Form SS4 @ the IRS.)

The decedent's final Federal income tax return (Form 1040) must be filed by April 15 of the year following the year of death. If necessary, the estate's administrator should request an automatic 6-month extension of time to file by filing Form 4868 on or before the tax return filing due date, i.e., the same April 15. Note, however, that Form 4868 need not be filed if there is no tax owing. The states in which decedent resided and/or owned income producing property will also require filing of state income tax returns.

If an (unofficial) administrator expects a Federal tax refund and there is no surviving spouse or court-appointed representative, Form 1310 (Statement of Person Claiming Refund Due a Deceased Person) should be filed together with the decedent's tax 1040 return.

The administrator must also be aware that the estate is treated as a separate taxpayer by tax authorities and is required to file income tax returns (Form 1041) on behalf of the estate when the estate receives income. For example, interest and investment income earned from invested assets held in the estate and earned and received after decedent's death is taxable income to the estate. (Note: income belonging to decedent before his/her death is income should be declared as income on decedent's final tax return.)

Estate returns are due and should be filed, unless extended, within three and a half (3 ½) months after the end of the estate's tax year. Estates can elect a fiscal year but that year must end no more than 11 months after date of death.

The administrator also needs to determine whether an Estate Tax Return (IRS Form 706) and Gift Tax Return (Form 709 - Generation-Skipping Transfer) will have to be prepared and filed. As indicated previously, the need to file a Form 706 will depend upon the size of decedent's estate.

For estates with assets more than a certain amount. Even though not every estate with assets over that amount will have an estate tax, those estates are still required to file. The Form 709 Gift Tax Return has to be filed if decedent made gifts worth more than $13,000 (or $26,000 in conjunction with a spouse) to any one person in his/her last year. These returns must be filed (unless extended) within nine (9) months after date of death. If there is good cause, the filing date may be extended for six (6) months.

Finally, if payments amounting to more than $600 are paid to professionals or non-corporate entities assisting the administrator (e.g., attorneys or accountants), the administrator should file a Form 1099-MISC (for each professional). Copies of such forms should be sent to the payees by January 31st of the year following the applicable tax year; the forms should be filed with the IRS no later than February 28 of that year (March 31 if filing electronically).

―――――――――――――

TAX FORMS YOU MAY NEED

Internal Revenue Service Forms

❖ Notice Concerning Fiduciary Relationship (Form 56)
❖ Request for U.S. Taxpayer ID Number and Certification (Form W9)
❖ U. S. Estate Tax Return (Form 706)
❖ U. S. Gift Tax Return (Form 709)
❖ U. S. Short Form Gift Tax Return (Form 709-A)
❖ Life Insurance Statement (Form 712)
❖ U. S. Individual Income Tax Return (Form 1040 or Form 1040A)
❖ Estimated Tax for Individuals (Form 1040-ES)
❖ Amended U. S. Individual Income Tax Return (Form 1040X)
❖ U. S. Fiduciary Income Tax Return (Form 1041 with K-l)
❖ Application for Tentative Refund (Form 1045)
❖ Application for Extension of Time for Payment of Tax (Form 1127)
❖ Statement of Person Claiming Refund for Deceased Taxpayer (Form 1310)
❖ Underpayment of Estimated Tax (Form 2210)
❖ Application for Additional Extension of Time to File (Form 2688)
❖ Application for Extension of Time to File (Form 2758)
❖ Power of Attorney and Declaration of Representative (Form 2848)
❖ Request for Copy of Tax Form (Form 4506)
❖ Application for Extension of Time to File U. S. Estate Tax Return and/or Pay Estate Tax (Form 4768)
❖ Application for Automatic Extension of Time to File Tax Return (Form 4868)
❖ Investment Interest Expense Deduction (Form 4952)
❖ Alternative Minimum Tax-Individuals (Form 6251)
❖ Passive Activity Loss Limitations (Form 8582)
❖ Home Mortgage Interest (Form 8598)
❖ Nondeductible IRA Contributions, IRA Basis, and Nontaxable IRA Distributions (Form 8606)
❖ Tax on Amounts Held in Account for Another
❖ Allocation of Decedent's Share of Income Tax (NAR Form 3-212)

Typical State Tax Forms

(names are functional and vary by state)

❖ Estate Tax Form (Federal Estate Tax Credit Form)
❖ Succession or Inheritance Tax Return
❖ Amendment to Succession Tax Return
❖ Affidavit in Nonresident Cases (e.g., for ancillary probate cases)
❖ Estate Income Tax Return
❖ Amended Estate Income Tax Form
❖ Application for Extension and Tentative Estate Income Tax Return
❖ Capital Gains, Dividends and Interest Income Tax Return
❖ Capital Gains, Dividends and Interest Income Tax Advance Payment or Request for Extension
❖ Local Real Estate Tax Forms

TYPICAL PROBATE FORMS

(This is a functional list. Actual names will vary by state)

1. General Waiver of Beneficiaries to Appointment of Fiduciary

2. Application/Administration or Probate of Will – Regular Form or Small Estate Form

3. Application/Ancillary Probate of Will

4. Affidavit in Filing Will not Submitted for Probate

5. Application/Decree and Return to Open Safe Deposit Box

6. Affidavit in Proof of Will and/or Codicil

7. Application and Decree for Support Allowance (for surviving dependents)

8. Affidavit in Lieu of Administration

9. Affidavit of Closing of Decedent's Estate

10. Return and List of Claims

11. Cover Sheet/Administration Account - Decedent's Estate

12. Decedent's Estate Administration Account

13. Statement in Lieu of Account

14. Acceptance of Trust/Ex Parte Decree for Qualified Testamentary Trustee

15. Waiver of Bond

17. Application to Sell or Mortgage Real Property

18. Affidavit of Financial Responsibility - Personal Surety

19. Inventory

20. Fiduciary's Periodic or Final Account

21. Probate Bond

22. Return of Sale or Mortgage of Real Property

23. Appt. of Judge of Probate as Agent for Service by Non-Resident Fiduciary

24. Application/Removal of Guardian

25. Application for Immediate Temporary Custody of Dependent (Child)

26. Application for Temporary Custody of Dependent (Child)

27. Application for Appointment of Guardian of Estate

28. Receipt and Release of Guardian of Estate

29. Certificate of Notice for Land Records

ABOUT THE AUTHOR

Neil J. Boyer is a practicing attorney in Wheaton, Illinois, where he advises clients regarding estate and financial planning and administration, organizations (for profit and not for profit; corporate, LLC, partnership, joint venture), transactions (e.g., acquisitions, sales, leasing, licensing, etc.), real estate, intellectual property, marketing and advertising.

As Adjunct Professor of Business with Argosy University and Adjunct Professor of Law at Fairfield University, he taught undergraduate and graduate courses in business law, strategic planning, marketing, and operations management, as well as estate planning and probate, charitable trusts, taxation, real estate and business law.

He has held senior executive positions with major organizations include: National Director of Planned Gifts at Alzheimer's Association, Assistant General Counsel of Rotary International and The Rotary Foundation's; and Vice President of International Sales and Marketing at Pullman International, a Fortune 500 company.

He is a frequent speaker at professional conferences and other forums and has published dissertations and articles on various topics, including estate planning and administration, long term care protection, and testimony before Congress on business related legislation.

Mr. Boyer holds a Doctor of Laws (J.D.) from the University of Illinois, a Masters of Science in Management (M.S. - Sloan Fellow) from MIT, and a Bachelors of Arts (B.A.) from Northwestern University.

In addition to being licensed to practice law before the bars of Illinois and Connecticut, he has held state and federal licenses in the insurance, securities, and real estate industries.

www.ingramcontent.com/pod-product-compliance
Lightning Source LLC
Chambersburg PA
CBHW081236170526
45165CB00009B/3073